BRITANNICA BEGINNER BIOS

LUDWIG VAN BEETHOVEN
COMPOSER OF THE CLASSICAL AND ROMANTIC ERAS

JEFF MAPUA

Britann
Educational Publis
IN ASSOCIATION W
ROSE
EDUCATIONAL SERVICES

Published in 2016 by Britannica Educational Publishing (a trademark of Encyclopædia Britannica, Inc.) in association with The Rosen Publishing Group, Inc.
29 East 21st Street, New York, NY 10010

Distributed exclusively by Rosen Publishing.
To see additional Britannica Educational Publishing titles, go to rosenpublishing.com.

First Edition

Britannica Educational Publishing
J. E. Luebering: Director, Core Reference Group
Mary Rose McCudden: Editor, Britannica Student Encyclopedia

Rosen Publishing
Hope Lourie Killcoyne: Executive Editor
Jacob R. Steinberg: Editor
Nelson Sá: Art Director
Michael Moy: Designer
Cindy Reiman: Photography Manager

Library of Congress Cataloging-in-Publication Data

Mapua, Jeff.
Ludwig van Beethoven: composer of the classical and romantic eras/Jeff Mapua.—First edition.
        pages cm.—(Britannica beginner bios)
Includes bibliographical references and index.
ISBN 978-1-62275-931-6 (library bound)—ISBN 978-1-62275-932-3 (pbk.)—ISBN 978-1-62275-934-7 (6-pack)
1. Beethoven, Ludwig van, 1770-1827—Juvenile literature. 2. Composers—Austria—Biography—Juvenile literature. I. Title.
ML3930.B4M36 2015
780.92—dc23
[B]
                                                                                    2014039762

Manufactured in the United States of America

Photo credits: Cover, pp. 13, 16, 19, 21 DEA/A. Dagli Orti/De Agostini/Getty Images; p. 1, interior pages (background) Ensuper/Shutterstock.com; p. 4 © iStockphoto/Thinkstock; p. 6 Three Lions/Hulton Archive/Getty Images; p. 8 (top) Culture Club/Hulton Archive/Getty Images; p. 8 (bottom) Bridgeman Images; p. 9 Private Collection/Bridgeman Images; p. 10 SuperStock/Getty Images; p. 11 DEA Picture Library/Getty Images; pp. 15, 24 Imagno/Hulton Archive/Getty Images; p. 17 Private Collection/Roger-Viollet, Paris/Bridgeman Images; p. 22 Gianni Dagli Orti/The Art Archive at Art Resource, NY; p. 23 Private Collection/Ken Welsh/Bridgeman Images; p. 27 Keith Hamshere/Moviepix/Getty Images; p. 28 S. Vannini/De Agostini Picture Library/Getty Images.

CONTENTS

ONE OF MUSIC'S GREATEST COMPOSERS

Ludwig van Beethoven was a composer, or somebody who writes music. He is often considered the greatest composer who ever lived. He created new ways of playing **CLASSICAL MUSIC**. For

Ludwig van Beethoven wrote music that expressed his feelings.

example, he created longer pieces that did more than just entertain listeners. Beethoven's music also expressed important ideas and deep feelings. His music expressed great energy and spirit. Beethoven's new form of classical music affected how other composers made music and how people valued music.

His Career

In the late 1700s, Beethoven became popular as a highly skilled piano player. Wealthy people in Europe enjoyed his music.

Quick Fact

Beethoven once said the feelings in his music came to him as "tones that sound, roar, and storm about me until I have [written] them down in notes."

Beethoven wrote many musical works for the piano.

Because of Beethoven, more people respected classical music. Beethoven helped establish music as an important area of the arts.

Loss of Hearing

In the late 1790s, Beethoven began to lose his hearing. By 1819 Beethoven had become totally deaf. He continued to create MASTERPIECES however. His works are still performed nearly two centuries after his death.

Vocabulary

Works done with great skill, especially ones that express great ideas or artistic achievement, are considered MASTERPIECES.

6

A YOUNG BOY WITH TALENT

Beethoven wrote nine **SYMPHONIES**, one **OPERA**, and many pieces for small groups and for piano and other instruments. At a young age Beethoven showed that he had a talent for music. With his family's help as well as years of education and hard work Beethoven developed his talent.

Vocabulary

SYMPHONIES are long pieces of music for many musicians to play together in an orchestra. An **OPERA** is a play in which usually the entire text is sung along to music played by an orchestra.

Early Childhood and Family Life

Ludwig van Beethoven was born in Bonn, Germany, in December 1770. He was the oldest child of Johann and Maria Magdalena van Beethoven. There were many musicians in the Beethoven family. Both Ludwig's father and grandfather were musicians in a royal court in Bonn.

When Ludwig was born, the Beethoven family had enough money to live well. However, in 1773 Ludwig's grandfather died and the family grew poor. Ludwig ended up leaving school at

Bonn, Germany, is a city along the Rhine, a river that runs through Switzerland, Germany, and the Netherlands. The house where Ludwig van Beethoven was born still stands in Bonn. Today it is an important museum.

age 11 to become a court organist. By the time he was 18, Ludwig supported his entire family with the money he earned from his work.

Court musicians were musicians who played for royalty at events such as parties and weddings.

It was his father, Johann, who gave Ludwig his early musical training. Johann made Ludwig practice all the time. He sometimes would even wake his son up in the middle of the night to practice.

Quick Fact

Beethoven spent his youth practicing the piano, violin, and French horn.

Following Mozart's Path

Johann saw that his son had a talent for the piano. He wanted Ludwig to be a famous young musician like Wolfgang Amadeus Mozart. Mozart was a famous composer who was known for being a child **PRODIGY**. Ludwig was not a prodigy, but he did study and become a more talented musician with time.

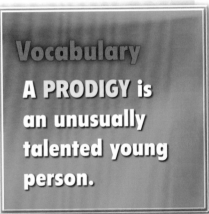

Ludwig learned musical writing from Christian Gottlob Neefe, the official organist in a royal court. He became Neefe's assistant at age 11 and

Vocabulary

A PRODIGY is an unusually talented young person.

Mozart wrote influential music and was famous when Beethoven was growing up.

Gottlob Neefe was one of Beethoven's music teachers.

published his first musical composition soon after.

As a teenager, Ludwig began to be successful. When he was 17, he was invited to the city of Vienna to study with Mozart. Little evidence can be found of a meeting between the two composers. However, a popular story says that the young Beethoven did play the piano for Mozart, and that Mozart was stunned by Beethoven's talent. Beethoven's visit to Vienna was cut short by news of his mother's death.

CHAPTER THREE

FIRST STEPS TO FAME

After returning to his hometown of Bonn, Beethoven remained there for five years. During that time he continued to work as a court musician. He also met many other great musicians who would help him develop his own style. He met important **ARISTOCRATS** who hired him to teach their children.

Return to Vienna

As Beethoven's fame in Bonn grew, more people heard about his talents. In

Vocabulary

ARISTOCRATS are members of families with money and power.

1790, a great composer named Franz Joseph Haydn noticed Beethoven. Haydn traveled through Bonn on his way to London. He offered to take on Beethoven as a student after returning from London.

In the fall of 1792, Beethoven left Bonn to return to Vienna, where he would study with Haydn. He would never return to Bonn again. In 1793, Haydn wrote a

Haydn was a great Austrian composer who taught Beethoven.

Quick Fact

Music was not just for people who worked as musicians in Vienna in the 1790s. Many aristocrats also studied and played instruments.

letter in which he said Beethoven would become "one of Europe's greatest composers."

Other Teachers

When he arrived in Vienna, Beethoven was already very popular. In 1791, Mozart had died. Many aristocrats in Vienna saw Beethoven as the next great composer.

Beethoven was talented, but he still needed to work hard to become great. There were certain problems with the way he wrote music that he wanted to fix. However, his teacher Haydn could not help him fix all of these problems. Beethoven continued studying with Haydn, but he also took other lessons in secret.

One of his secret teachers was the organist Johann Georg Albrechtsberger. He helped improve Beethoven's technique, or performance of skills. Antonio Salieri, the royal music director, taught Beethoven how to

Johann Georg Albrechtsberger helped Beethoven become a better musician.

write music that included words and song. In 1794, Haydn traveled again to London, leaving Beethoven on his own.

First Period Work

Beethoven's music changed over time. It has been divided into three time periods. His first period lasted from 1794 until about 1800. During that time, he created music that sounded much like other classical music at that time. Beethoven's first public appearance playing piano in Vienna happened in 1795.

This picture shows the Hofburg theater in Vienna, Austria, where Beethoven first performed a public concert. The theater is now called the Burgtheater.

He played a **CONCERTO** (no. 2, Opus 19) of his own and one by Mozart. Beethoven also took part in a benefit concert for Haydn. Even more important, his *Three Trios for Piano, Violin, and Cello*, Opus 1 were published.

Over the next three years Beethoven traveled to play music in the cities of Berlin and Prague. In 1800, he launched an important public concert.

Vocabulary

A CONCERTO is a piece for one or more main musicians with an orchestra. It usually has three movements, or parts.

His piano con-
certi, the *Septet*
(Opus 20) and the
First Symphony
were performed.
The event helped
spread his fame in
other countries.

Most of
Beethoven's works
during the first
period were for the
piano. He began using
other instruments in
his compositions while still creating masterpieces for
the piano.

This is the original sheet music to one of Beethoven's works.

CHAPTER FOUR

SUCCESS AND CHALLENGES

In the late 1790s, Beethoven began to lose his hearing. For some time he continued to compose and perform as before. However his condition eventually changed his life—and the way he wrote music.

Becoming Deaf

Beethoven began to lose his hearing before he was 30 years old. At first, his life was not affected much. He continued to play music in public and to compete with other pianists, or piano players. However, by 1802 Beethoven was sure that his hearing would only get worse. He also had severe pain in the area around his stomach.

Beethoven spent the summer of 1802 in the country-side. He wrote to his two brothers about how his condition made him feel. He began to lose hope and feel sad. How-ever, Beethoven's love of music kept him going. He refused to quit making music, even though it would be much harder for him without his hearing.

For the rest of his life Beethoven searched for a cure to make him feel better. The pain in his stomach did not go away. Beethoven did not com-pletely lose his hearing until

A young Beethoven from about 1802 is shown.

Quick Fact

Beethoven worked on more than one composition at a time and was not in a hurry to finish them. For example, he started working on his famous *Fifth Symphony* in 1804 but did not finish it until 1808!

1819. After that, Beethoven's friends would write down questions, and Beethoven would say his answers aloud to them.

As he could no longer play live, Beethoven spent more of his time writing new music. He still appeared in public from time to time. Many of his musical ideas came to him on long walks and were noted in sketchbooks.

Second Period Work

Around the time that Beethoven began to lose his hearing, he started creating a different style of music. He continued writing music in this new style until 1814.

This time period is often called Beethoven's second period of work. His compositions sounded similar in some ways to the **IMPROVISATION** he had been famous for during performances. The music had surprising rhythms and feeling. His works became different from other classical music at the time. For example, the first and second movements in his works became shorter, whereas his third and final movements became longer. His final movements, or finales, were very strong. At times

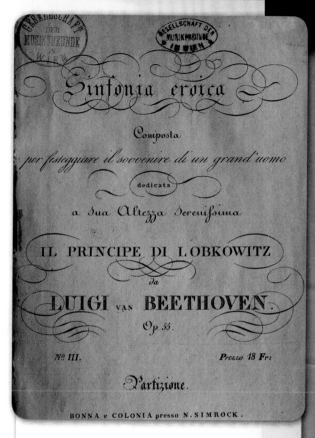

Beethoven's *Third Symphony* is also called the *Eroica*.

Beethoven's finale would be the most important part of an entire piece. Some of Beethoven's most famous works, such as the *Eroica* (1804) symphony and the *Fourth Piano Concerto* (1806), were written during the second period.

Personal Life

Beethoven had a temper, and his mood could quickly change. During his years in Vienna, he had many friends, but he still wrote about feeling lonely. His wealthy friends supported him with money.

Beethoven was in love with several women during this period. He dedicated his very famous piano work *Moonlight Sonata* (1801) to a countess named Giulietta Guicciardi,

Josephine Brunsvik was one of the women whom Beethoven loved during his second period of work.

who married another man. He later proposed marriage to Guicciardi's cousin Josephine Brunsvik as well as another woman named Therese Malfatti. However, he never got married.

After Beethoven's death, secret letters were found. These letters were addressed to someone whom Beethoven called his **IMMORTAL** Beloved. The letters were love notes. To this day people do not know with certainty who this person was.

Vocabulary

Something IMMORTAL lasts or lives forever.

Pictured is one of many love notes that Beethoven wrote to a woman whom he called his Immortal Beloved.

CHAPTER FIVE

FINAL YEARS AND GIFT TO THE WORLD

Beethoven's third (and final) period of work lasted from 1814 until the end of his life. It had a wider range of **HARMONY**. In 1824, he performed his *Ninth Symphony* with great success. Because he was completely deaf at that point, Beethoven did not know that the listeners were clapping until one of the

The Theater am Kärntnertor in Vienna, Austria, is where Beethoven performed his *Ninth Symphony* in 1824.

musicians made him turn to face the audience.

The *Ninth Symphony* was Beethoven's last major work. It is often considered his greatest composition.

Vocabulary
HARMONY is the combination of musical notes played together as chords.

It is an unusually long piece of music that takes more than one hour to perform. It also is unusual because it requires a very large orchestra to play it. The last movement includes a full choir, or group of singers. The choir sings a theme called "Ode to Joy." It is a powerful and very grand finale. The *Ninth Symphony* greatly influenced later music. Many composers started using large orchestras and choirs in ways similar to the way Beethoven did in that work.

What Made Him Sick?

Beethoven died in Vienna on March 26, 1827. Twenty thousand people attended his funeral! While he was alive, no one knew why Beethoven had gone deaf, what made his stomach hurt, or why his mood often changed.

Scientists still do not have a definite answer for why Beethoven died. Some tests on Beethoven's hair and bones showed signs of lead poisoning. (Lead is a metal that is poisonous to humans.) Scientists thought that lead poisoning could have caused Beethoven's stomach pains, bad temper, and sadness. However, later tests on his hair and bones did not show signs of lead poisoning. Scientists also wonder if Beethoven died because of problems with his liver.

What He Gave the World

Beethoven's music had a great effect on other classical music composers of the 1800s. Some of the most famous composers from this period after Beethoven's death were Peter Tchaikovsky and Johannes Brahms.

Beethoven's early compositions were in the classical style. He later burst forth with a new style of music. He used clashing chords called **DISSONANCE** in a way that was shocking in his day.

Beethoven's music has been used in many films and television shows. There have also been movies made about Beethoven. The movies *Immortal Beloved* (1994) and *Copying Beethoven* (2006) are about his life.

Before Beethoven, music without vocals was commonly

Actor Gary Oldman played Beethoven in the movie *Immortal Beloved* (1994).

Vocabulary

DISSONANCE is a clashing of notes that gives an unstable feeling. In music, dissonance is often followed by notes that do not clash and give a stable feeling, to resolve the clashing sound.

seen as less important than music with vocals. After Beethoven, many consider instrumental music to be the highest level of art.

Remembering Beethoven

Beethoven has stayed popular even centuries after his death. His masterpieces are still performed today. New composers continue to be influenced by Beethoven's unique sound. Generations of new fans continue to be moved by Beethoven's life story and his music.

The Beethoven Memorial Museum in Martonvasar, Hungary, pays tribute to the great composer.

1770: Ludwig van Beethoven is born in Bonn, Germany, in December.

1773: Beethoven's grandfather dies.

1782: In June, Beethoven becomes Christian Gottlob Neefe's assistant as court organist.

1783: Beethoven is appointed continuo player to the Bonn opera.

1787: Beethoven possibly meets Wolfgang Amadeus Mozart.

1787: Beethoven's mother, Maria Magdalena van Beethoven, dies on July 17.

1790: Composer Franz Joseph Haydn first notices Beethoven.

1792: In the fall, Beethoven accepts Haydn's offer to study composition with him.

1792: Beethoven's father, Johann van Beethoven, dies.

1794–1800: Beethoven's first period of music, known for mostly piano compositions and early improvisation.

1795: On March 29 Beethoven makes his first public appearance in Vienna.

1796: The first signs of Beethoven's deafness begin to appear.

1800: Beethoven gives a large public concert in Vienna.

1801–1814: Beethoven's second period.

1814–1827: Beethoven's third period of music, during which time Beethoven goes completely deaf.

1819: Beethoven becomes totally deaf.

1826: Beethoven becomes sick with a lung disease called pneumonia.

1827: Beethoven dies on March 26, in Vienna, Austria.

GLOSSARY

COMPOSITION A written piece of music and especially one that is very long and involved.

COURT The residence of a ruler, especially of a king or queen.

INFLUENTIAL Having the power to cause changes.

ORCHESTRA A group of musicians who play instruments together and who are led by a conductor.

ORGANIST Someone who plays an organ.

PERIOD A stage or portion of time in the history of something.

RHYTHM A regular, repeated pattern of sounds.

TECHNIQUE The manner in which details are treated or basic skills are performed.

VOCALS Parts that are sung.

BOOKS

Bauer, Helen. *Beethoven for Kids: His Life and Music with 21 Activities.* Chicago, IL: Chicago Review Press, 2011.

Carew-Miller, Anna. *Ludwig van Beethoven: Great Composer.* Broomall, PA: Mason Crest, 2013.

DK Publishing. *Children's Book of Music.* London, England: DK Publishing, 2010.

Machajewski, Sarah. *Musical Genius: Ludwig van Beethoven.* New York, NY: Rosen Classroom, 2014.

Martin, Russell, and Lydia Nibley. *The Mysteries of Beethoven's Hair.* Watertown, MA: Charlesbridge, 2009.

WEBSITES

Because of the changing nature of Internet links, Rosen Publishing has developed an online list of websites related to the subject of this book. This site is updated regularly. Please use this link to access this list:

http://www.rosenlinks.com/BBB/Beet

INDEX